NOT BY BREAD ALONE

Fifty-Two Weekly Reflections on
the Matters that Matter Most

By Richard M. Gray

WestBow
PRESS
A DIVISION OF THOMAS NELSON

WestBow Press books may be ordered through booksellers or by contacting:

WestBow Press
A Division of Thomas Nelson
1663 Liberty Drive
Bloomington, IN 47403
www.westbowpress.com
1-(866) 928-1240

Because of the dynamic nature of the Internet, any web addresses or links contained in this book may have changed since publication and may no longer be valid. The views expressed in this work are solely those of the author and do not necessarily reflect the views of the publisher, and the publisher hereby disclaims any responsibility for them.

Any people depicted in stock imagery provided by Thinkstock are models, and such images are being used for illustrative purposes only. Certain stock imagery © Thinkstock.

Qoute in introduction from Jesus: A Biograhy from a Believer by Paul Johnson used by permission of Viking Penguin, a division of Penguin Group (USA), Inc.

ISBN: 978-1-4497-7082-2 (e)
ISBN: 978-1-4497-7081-5 (sc)
Library of Congress Control Number: 2012918951

Printed in the United States of America

WestBow Press rev. date: 3/6/2013

INTRODUCTION

"IN THE BEGINNING WAS THE WORD." That's the opening statement of the Gospel of John. *Word*, of course, is a translation of the Greek *Logos*, which meant the sustaining order of things. But it also goes back to the Hebrew understanding of the *Word of the Lord*, in which God's *Word* had *power* to effect its purpose in the world.

Even today, when we're so immersed in meaningless words we take them lightly, we can still believe the Spirit's *Word* has the power to effect change. Hence the reflections in this book on the Word, God's *poetic* word..

There are many ways to communicate the truths we discern from the Spirit. The Bible itself contains a large array of such ways, from historical narratives to laws, from stories to proverbs, songs to parables and, in the case of the Hebrew prophets, even strange and surprising actions.

There may be no medium with such *expressive economy*, however, as the medium of poetry.

In his letter to the Ephesians, the apostle Paul wrote "We are God's workmanship, created in Christ Jesus for good works." And the meaning of the Greek word for "workmanship" is *poema*, from which we derive the word "poem." We are, in short, God's own poetic creations.

And what about Jesus of Nazareth? Paul Johnson, in *Jesus: A Biography from a Believer*, writes that "The truth is, Jesus was not so much a rhetorician, or a preacher, as a poet. He thought and reasoned and spoke as a poet does — in images, flashes of insight and metaphors from the world of nature. All the time he taught he was creating little pictures in the minds of the men and women who listened to him. He was the poet of virtue, the bard of righteousness, the minstrel of divine love."

No-one can claim ultimate truth or wisdom. These lie quite beyond our grasp. All we can do, when we think we're inspired ("breathed into") by the Spirit, is to serve as faithful if fallible spokespersons for that Spirit. We can discern whether our words are faithful or not when, as Paul writes, "the Spirit witnesses with our own spirit" that our words (at least some of them) are truly the voice of the Spirit.

The title of the book comes from Jesus' temptations in the wilderness. Having fasted for forty days, he was hungry. And the tempter came and said to him, "If you are the Son of God, command these stones to become loaves of bread." But he answered, "It is written that man shall not live by bread alone, but by every word that proceeds from the mouth of God."

The themes of the poems herein, which can be seen as both a catalog of our hopes and a record of our times, have been drawn from three sources. They were either:

1. Inspired by Scripture
2. Torn from the Headlines (or Timely Books) or
3. Discovered in Contemplation

Fifty-two of them follow, each with a brief prose commentary, enough at the rate of one each week to take the reader through the year.

TABLE OF CONTENTS

INSPIRED BY SCRIPTURE

What's In a Name?

Moses said to God, "If I come to the people of Israel and say to them 'The God of your fathers has sent me to you, and they ask me, 'What is his name?' what shall I say to them?" God said to Moses, "I AM Who I AM. Say this to the people, 'I AM has sent me to you."

This enigmatic answer by the Nameless One is preceded by the promise that the way Moses will know that God has called him is that he (Moses) will return from Egypt with his people and worship God "upon this mountain." The "sign," therefore, that Moses has been called will be his carrying out the mission. Not the most reassuring of signs.

Then when Jesus appeared, many hundreds of years later, he used this same enigmatic name in reference to himself. This was blasphemy. It was this name as much as his cleansing of the Temple that resulted in his crucifixion.

Whatever else it means, it is clear that I AM is the God not just of creation but also of history, the God who acts in human affairs.

I AM

I Am, the Galilean said.
Knowing he needed say no more
Than these the words that Moses heard
Beside the bush, so long before.

This was the name the nameless one
Had given as a guarantee
That he would be their sovereign Lord
Through time and all eternity.

And now the one who called himself
The Son of Man had come to be
The incarnation of that pledge
To all of those who would be free.

Free from the dull disquietude
That tempers every human breath,
Free from the greed that chokes its children,
Free from the awesome fear of death.

What did it mean, this cryptic phrase?
Was it meant to mask a mystery
That those constrained by time and space
Can scarcely know, or feel, or see?

Or was it simply an invitation
To live within his loving care?
A message sealed in sacrifice,
The promise that I will be there.

A COVENANT IS FOREVER

THE Old Covenant ("Testament" in Latin) is "old" only in the sense that it predates what Christians call the "New" Covenant (or New Testament), not in the sense that the old is superseded by the new.

A covenant made by God is irrevocable; it is made once for all. Even Jeremiah's prophecy, "Behold, the days are coming, says the Lord, when I will make a new covenant with the House of Israel and the House of Judah," is new only in that it is "unlike the covenant I made with their fathers when I took them by the hand to bring them out of the land of Egypt."

What is the nature of the new covenant? That it is no longer *external* (i.e. simply taught by others) but rather *internal*. "I will put my law within them, and I will write it upon their hearts. No longer shall each man teach his neighbor and each his brother, for they shall all know me, from the least of them to the greatest, for I will forgive their iniquity, and I will remember their sin no more."

The "old" covenant is still in force!

HEAR, O ISRAEL

Hear, O Israel, once for all,
The joy and burden of your call:
The Lord your God, the Lord is One,
And you shall love Him like a son,
With all your heart, and mind, and soul,
Fit for your mission, cleansed and whole.
Remember, Israel, it was He
Who from your bondage set you free.
He brought you to a promised land,
And taught you there to understand
That you were His so you might be
A light for all the world to see.
If the living God called Abraham friend,
His covenant will never end.
It stands in perpetuity
Until the end of history!

In the Morning, Gladness

From A to Z -- anger to zeal -- almost every human emotion can be found in the Psalms, which subjectively reflect every hope and fear of the human heart. But the chief emotion expressed in the Psalms, literally scores of times, is that of *joy* -- especially joy in the presence of God. And this joy is often preceded by a sense of hopelessness or despair.

"Weeping may tarry for the night," Psalm 30 reads, "but joy comes in the morning."

A strong element in the joyful thanksgiving of the Psalms is the knowledge and certainty that God has been, and continues to be, at work in the history of his people, Israel.

Finally, along with joy are the psalmist's inexpressible yearnings of the human spirit for union with the Spirit of God, which has produced some of the most poignant and moving poetry in history.

FROM TEARS TO JOY

(THE PSALMS REVISITED)

We have wept alone in silence, Lord.
We have known regret, dismay, despair.
But we cannot flee your tireless Word.
Be in hell or heaven, you are there.

How would it serve you if our souls
Were shattered and consumed in shame?
Who in the depths of hell extols
Your wondrous grace or hails your name?

Is it the measure of that grace,
Which all who trust you know so well,
That you should meet us face to face
Even in the depths of hell?

As the doe longs for flowing streams,
Our spirits long for you, O Lord.
You are the One whose love redeems
Us from life's chaos and discord.

You are the One whose cleansing light
Transfigures sadness, pain, and sorrow,
Turning the tears we shed tonight
Into the gladness of tomorrow.

IN WHAT SHALL WE TRUST?

THE prophet Jeremiah said it better than anyone: "Let not the wise man glory in his wisdom, let not the mighty man glory in his might, let not the rich man glory in his riches; but let him who glories glory in this, that he understands and knows me, that I am the Lord who practice kindness, justice, and righteousness in the earth; for in these things I delight, says the Lord."

As human beings we choose, to a large degree, the source of meaning in our lives by choosing the commitments we make, i.e. the "ultimate concern" in which we place our trust. Martin Luther once said that the human mind is a factory busy manufacturing idols, and there are certainly no idols more attractive than wisdom, power, and wealth.

In the face of these options, Jeremiah holds up the living God and says to Israel, put your trust in Him.

ON TRUSTING

To live is but to learn to choose
The purpose of our life's design;
To signify in graphic hues
That faith to which our hearts incline.

Some trust in wisdom -- chaste, austere,
And understanding -- wisdom's prize,
But history makes one canon clear:
God's ways are foolish to the wise.

Some trust in power -- in fire and steel,
Yet strangely, time and time again,
God chooses weakness to repeal
The proud, imperious power of men.

Some trust in wealth to help forestall
The awesome anguish death inspires.
But wealth cannot save life at all,
And death takes all of wealth's desires.

So let us raise a grateful prayer
To Him who makes His purpose known
By giving us a Son -- and Heir --
That we may trust in him alone!

The Face of God

WHAT would God be like if God had a human face? Perhaps like the vision of the prophet Ezekiel in which God seems to be "like the human one," whom Ezekiel calls the "Son of Man" (idiomatically the " Human Being") some 93 times.

The possibility of incarnation is not exclusive to the New Testament. Walter Wink writes in his book, *The Human Being*, that "in Ezekiel, we see God becoming closer to humanity, seeking incarnation, while in (the book of) Daniel we see humanity approaching God, seeking transformation. The offspring of this mutual attraction is the Human Being."

The remarkable fact about the incarnation, then, in the words of John's gospel, is that "No one has ever seen God; the only Son, who is in the bosom of the Father, he has made him known."

Jesus, then, is the human face that God has given to humankind.

NIGHT'S END

Quietly, expectantly,
Although the night is far from gone,
We watch and wait, intent to see
The coming of your promised dawn.

We groan within to hear your Word.
Our natures yearn to know your Name..
Our hearts attend like candles, Lord.
Your living Spirit is the flame.

Unveil for us that shining place,
Unwearied by the world's alarms,
Where earth meets heaven, face to face,
Encircled by a mother's arms.

A place where flesh and spirit dwell
In unashamed simplicity,
Though pilgrim-kings will come to tell
Their own amazed epiphany.

Like them we come in faith to find
The focus of our soul's delight --
The One who brings to humankind
In every age, the end of night!

ON DARKNESS AND LIGHT

FROM the beginning of Genesis to the end of Revelation, light symbolizes the presence of God. Creation itself is seen as the separation of darkness and light. So it is not surprising that John the Baptist identifies Jesus as the "light of men," or that Jesus calls himself (in the Gospel of John) "the light of the world."

Nor is it surprising that judgment is that "the light has come into the world, and men loved darkness rather than light, because their deeds were evil. For every one who does evil hates the light, and does not come to the light, lest his deeds should be exposed."

This unequivocal division between darkness and light marks the difference between life and death. The choice is optional but the consequences are not. Could there be any more stark decision for any human being?

OUT OF THE DARKNESS, LIGHT

Deep was the darkness, wide and deep,
That wrapped the world in fitful sleep.
Thick were the clouds of fear and doubt
That shut the heart's compassion out.

Lost were His people, all but gone
Their vision of the promised dawn.
Long had they known with every breath
That life was swallowed up in death.

Then, like the breaking light of day
That lifts the shroud of night away,
Came Christmas! Wondrous, glorious morn
When Christ, the Herald of Life, was born.

The shepherds and the sages came
To praise and magnify his name
While Mary in a manger laid
This one for whom the world was made.

The one above all earthly powers
Whose victory over death is ours,
The one in whom we finally see
God's power -- and God's humility!

THE UNKINGLY ONE

THERE is a recent computer game entitled *Empires: Dawn of the Modern World*, which takes place from 950 C.E. to 1950 C.E., in which players can lead a civilization to global domination.

While they didn't have PC's in their day, the Romans knew how to play that game. They were the unquestioned dominators of the world, in which every subject was subservient to the emperor; everyone, it seems, except the Christians, who worshipped a different kind of ruler.

It was no secret to the authorities that Jesus introduced a new kind of kingdom, the kingdom of God which was, in every respect, the antithesis of empire. The "blessed ones" were the disenfranchised -- the poor, the gentle, the peacemakers, the pure in heart, the persecuted. Could anyone doubt that these values were, in fact, a threat to the imperial system? And given that fact, could there have been any outcome other than Jesus' crucifixion?

While the emperor Constantine's "conversion" to Christianity made the Christian faith a tool -- and often an example --of empire, the Spirit has never permitted Jesus' "un-kingly" stance and behavior to be entirely lost to the world.

A DIFFERENT KIND OF KING

Surely they weren't kingly:
The stall, the straw, the earth.
What kind of king would condescend
To such a common birth?

Surely they weren't courtly:
His pin-pricks at the proud.
And would a king refuse a crown
Thrust on him by the crowd?

Surely it wasn't regal:
The way in which he died.
Stretched out upon a public cross,
A thief on either side.

And so the world says "Nonsense"
That his God, who let him fall,
Has raised him from a borrowed grave
And made him Lord of all.

Yet there's a voice that whispers
To depths within the soul,
"Behold! This is your Lord and king
Who died to make you whole."

And for each one who answers,
"My God! Emmanuel!"
His was the birthday of a king.
His was a glad Noel.

THE CHILD AS MODEL

"So he put a child in their midst and said, 'unless you become like children you will never enter the kingdom of heaven." Jesus was not praising childishness but rather the *child-likeness* which is the key to accepting God's sovereignty.

Nor did Elijah experience God in the wind, the earthquake, or fire, but in that "still, small voice" he heard in his cave on the mountaintop. Humility of heart and mind, it seems, is the *sine qua non* for entering God's fold.

This is not the world's way. The domination system that governs human affairs looks instead to power, but not the kind of power that finds its strength in weakness or the Christ-like power of innocence. The child as model of the kingdom is the paradox this verse seeks to address.

But Not a Child

Lord of the Heavens, by whose grace
The stars themselves are held beguiled,
Dwell in the vaulting tract of space
Somewhere, we pray, but not a child.

Lord of the earth, whose powers inspire
The tempest, raging dark and wild,
Speak through the earthquake, wind, and fire
As God and King! But not a child.

A child who grew in trust to see
Each bud and seed as tales to tell,
Each calling forth of life to be
His Father's work -- and his, as well.

A child who rose to manhood bound
Like us by nation, tribe, and race,
And yet whose love, unfettered, found
The world enclosed in its embrace.

A child whose birth the world ignored,
Whose life and work were scarcely known,
Whose shameful death, which few deplored,
Was suffered on the cross, alone.

And while believers yet contend
This "son of man" survives the grave,
We find it awkward to defend
A son who suffers like a slave.

We cannot understand, O Lord,
The kind of rule you would proclaim,
Declare your power and be adored!
But do not stoop to share this shame.

With firm and unrelenting hand,
Your judgment hurl from heav'n above,
We have the weapons to withstand
Your judgment, Lord, but not your love.

Manual for a Mission

How do you coach a savior? What kind of instruction would the living God give to the "son of man" (i.e. that human being) who is called to be a light to the nation which, in turn, has been called to be a light to the world?

What kind of reception should he expect? For what kind of testing should he be prepared? How can he communicate the nature and purpose of the living God?

What competencies, what courage, what character should be reflected in his mission as an itinerant rabbi who has "no place to lay his head"? The charge would be overwhelming were it not for the Holy Spirit.

Counsel

The appointed hour has come, my son,
To kindle fire upon the earth.
Be not dismayed that course to run
Which prophets told before your birth.

Embrace the outcast. Heal the ill.
Restore the lost. Support the weak.
The hungry and the thirsty fill.
With faith and hope empower the meek.

Persist upon the path of love,
Not counting what it costs to care.
Be singleminded as a dove,
Yet with a serpent's guile, beware.

Beware the ones who cling to fear,
Who will not let you set them free.
Not trusting, they will never hear.
Not hearing, they will not know me.

Stay clear of those who feel no pain,
Whose hearts shut out the world's distress.
Too late they turn to me in vain.
Who cannot weep, I cannot bless.

And most of all, my son, beware
The proud who claim a special place,
The righteous ones who cannot bear
The thought -- or gift -- of unearned grace.

But even if they kill, forgive.
For those who love, death has no sting.
As I am life, they too will live
And I will give them ... everything!

AND THE WORD BECAME FLESH …

Has there ever been, in the whole history of the human race, any greater or deeper mystery than that of the Incarnation?

In the Old Testament, the "Word" (in the Greek, *logos*), "reason," or "wisdom" of God was a form of divine revelation, the way that God communicated with human beings the knowledge of His will. So it is no surprise that the Gospel of John parallels the creation story in Genesis by stating that "In the beginning was the Word, and the Word was with God, and the Word was God." The real surprise follows with the message that "the Word became flesh and dwelt among us, full of grace and truth."

This is the Incarnation, the startling announcement that Jesus came forth from the being of God to realize God's purpose of "dwelling with men."

The church doctrine of the Trinity -- Father, Son, and Holy Spirit -- came much later, as did the debate at the Council of Nicaea in 325 C.E. sponsored by the Roman emperor Constantine as to whether Jesus was human (Arius) or divine (Athanasius), a debate which continues in some quarters today.

That debate does not detract for a moment, however, from the wonder or the mystery of the Incarnation.

GOD WITH US

When you say "I Am," do you mean
You are present every moment, Lord?
Present to every corner
Of creation every minute?
Present alike for protozoa
And the pulsing Pleiades?
Present for this blue-green earth
And every creature in it?

That thought is far too high for us.
Its scope is past our knowing.
The cosmic compass of your care
We cannot comprehend.
We cannot grasp the meaning
Of benevolence, it seems,
Unless it's in the simple
Loving-kindness of a friend.

And so we bless you for your Son
Who came as one of us,
His incarnation manifests
The measure of your grace.
That, bowing to the narrow
Limits of our understanding,
You let us see your great
Compassion fully, face to face.

What can we do then, Lord,
Except to bow in grateful praise,
Astounded by the promise
Of the story we would tell.
The story of your faithfulness,
The same from age to age,
That once upon a Christmas Day
He came -- Emmanuel!

The Audacity of the Gospel

THE only thing more audacious than the fact that God revealed his nature and character in a human being, Jesus of Nazareth, is the fact that this God knows, intimately, each and every one of us.

Yet this is the revelation of the One whom Jesus called *Abba* to every person who can truthfully answer Jesus' question, "Who do you say that I am?" with the affirmation: "You are the Christ, the son of the living God."

Jesus was not the first to speak of the personal care and compassion of God. Creation itself was seen as an expression of that care. The covenant that God made with Israel was a special expression of his compassion. And the voices of the prophets both deepened and clarified the intensity of God's love for his people.

If the prophets were the *messengers* of God's *chesed*, however, i.e. his sure and steadfast loving-kindness, Jesus himself was the *message* of that care in human form.

His followers knew that God cared because *Jesus* cared, even to the point of the shame and humiliation of death on the cross. His was the evidence of God's everlasting compassion. His was the guarantee that God sees and knows and cares not just for the world in general but for every one of his children in particular.

THE GOSPEL ON THE MOUNT

"YOUR FATHER SEES."
What hopes were stirred
By all the things those words convey,
And how transfixed were those who heard
Them on the mountainside that day.

"YOUR FATHER KNOWS."
Could that be true?
That all our hopes and needs are known?
That none of us in what we do
Is unremembered, lost, alone?

"YOUR FATHER CARES."
How long the earth
Had waited, yes, and yearned to hear
That warrant of the soul's self-worth
Which stills the heart's disabling fear.

So in due season, for the one
In whom the sovereign chose to dwell,
We bring our thanks that through the Son
We know the Father's love as well.

And falling at his feet disclose
Our faith, in simple, earnest prayer,
In Him who HEARS and SEES and KNOWS,
And holds us always in His care.

THE GREAT REVERSAL

Rich, proud, self-sufficient: these are qualities valued by the world. Then came the prophets and Jesus who turned conventional wisdom on its ear.

The poor, the humble, the sorrowful, the orphan, and the widow: these are the ones God favors and protects.

"Blessed are the poor in spirit," said Jesus in the Revised Standard translation of Matthew (simply "the poor" in Luke), "for theirs is the kingdom of heaven." Other translations are even more pointed. The Contemporary English Version: "God blesses those people who depend only on him." The New English Bible, capturing the Aramaic imperative, reads: "How blest are those who know their need of God."

If Jesus promises woe for the rich and the full, however, Friedrich Nietzsche promises power. In his doctrine of the superman (ubermensch), Nietzsche posits that selfishness is "blessed, wholesome, healthy" and that the lust to rule is a "gift-giving virtue." Small wonder that he became, for Hitler, the Nazi house philosopher. In like manner, Voltaire insisted that Christianity is the "most ridiculous, the most absurd, and bloody religion that has ever infected the world."

In the face of these and other detractors, the Beatitudes still stand as the manifesto of a caring God.

The Beatitudes Revisited

How blest are those who know their need
Of Him whose love sustains us all ...
God's rule is there.

How blest are those who weep when others
Suffer and who heed their call ...
They know His care.

The gentle-hearted, too, are blest.
To them he will entrust the land.
And all who yearn for right to prosper
Shall be fed by His own hand.

How blest the ones who have no need
To square accounts. His grace will be
Returned in kind.

And those whose lives are lived in simple
Faith and true sincerity
His joy will find.

The reconcilers, too, are blest,
Who heal men's wounds, so wars may cease.
They do His work who came to be
The servant of a reign of peace.

WHO IS THIS SON?

I<small>N</small> his seminal book, *The Human Being*, theologian Walter Wink explores the origin of the term, "son of man" (Jesus' reference to himself) in Ezekiel.

In answer to the question of what it means that God is revealed to Ezekiel as a human, Wink proposes that becoming human is the task that God has set for human beings, who do not know what it means to be human.

Since we scarcely know what humanness is, therefore, and are incapable of becoming human by ourselves, we are given the "son of man" (in non-sexist language, the human being).

We are not meant to be divine, in other words, which we cannot be, but to become what we truly are -- human. I would add that this is because, as in the case of Jesus, *authentic humanity is transparent to divinity.*

That is the point of this verse about "the Son of Man." There is no more sacred calling than joining Jesus in his community of the *human* beings.

THE HUMAN BEING

He called himself the "Son of Man,"
The truly Human one was he,
Challenging every unjust power
That dominates humanity.

Censuring systems based on class,
Religion, gender, tribe, or race,
He lived the reign of One who grants
Undifferentiated grace.

He gave the title "Son of Man"
To those who followed him as well,
Who came to see that they, like him,
Could stand against the gates of hell.

Like him they sought no great acclaim,
No glory, title, praise, or crown,
And yet before their work was done,
They turned the whole world upside down.

We would not know what "human" means
Nor what it is we're called to be
Except for Him whose life empowers
The human possibility.

So in the season of his birth
Let us proffer, as we can,
Our gratitude for God's great gift,
His *human* gift, the Son of Man!

A NEW MODEL FOR HUMANITY

THOMAS Kuhn, in *The Structure of Scientific Revolutions* (1962), popularized the term *paradigm shift*. The Copernican revolution, for example (the sun as the center of the solar system) was a paradigm shift from the Ptolemaic model of the earth as the system's center.

In the historical, theological world, Jesus of Nazareth, crucified as "king of the Jews," certainly represented a paradigm shift not only from the Jewish expectation of a conquering Messiah, or *anointed one* on the order of King David, but also for the entire human race with its understanding of power and its widespread systems of domination.

The author of Hebrews describes Jesus as "the pioneer and perfecter of our faith." For Christians everywhere he is the model of a new humanity, a radical shift in the order of what it means to be human.

PARADIGM SHIFT

Human Jesus, gentle Jew,
Our human arms reach out to you.
A king astride a stately steed
Is not the kind of guide we need,
But one whose great, triumphal day
Was signaled by a donkey's bray.

No privilege was yours to be
An earthly son of Galilee.
No deference did you demand;
No fearful force did you command.
Like us, you knew temptation's test,
And mockery was a constant guest.

But unlike us you chose, above
The way of self, the way of love.
Obedient to the one whose care
Surrounds His children everywhere,
You stayed that course until the end
As prophet, teacher, healer, friend.

And here we are, your siblings all,
Culture-bound, constrained, and small.
Travelers in a troubled land,
Where chaos waits at every hand,
We long to be your counterpart,
Well-girded with a generous heart.

But as we travel paths unknown,
We know we cannot walk alone,
And so we seek the One you knew,
To walk beside Him just like you,
And turn to you His norm to see
For true, transformed humanity.

THE EVERLASTING TRILOGY

IN the hymn to love in the apostle Paul's first letter to the church at Corinth, we find these words: "So faith, hope, love abide, these three, but the greatest of these is love."

Experience tells us that without faith and hope, however, it is difficult if not impossible to love, at least in the sense of *agape*, which refers to the will rather than to the emotion, and which, according to "A Theological Wordbook of the Bible," often conveys the idea of *showing* love in action.

The number of New Testament references to these three qualities seem to rank their importance. Hope appears 73 times, Faith 121, while Love outranks them both at 138 times (not to mention more than twice that number of references in the Old Testament).

A pastor we know makes the same point every Sunday: we can count on the living God loving us because God is love and "God cannot help being God."

We find the final word on love, however, in the first letter of John: "We love, because he first loved us."

REGENERATION

Whenever doubt subdues our minds
And leaves them bound in cynics' chains,
Some simple, unexplained event
Declares the Lord of *FAITH* still reigns!

Whenever death disarms our wills,
Constricting courage, feeding fear,
Some unexpected voice proclaims
The Lord of *HOPE* is always near!

Whenever self-absorption blinds
Our hearts to pressing human need,
Some gracious act of caring cries
The Lord of *LOVE* is Lord indeed!

And so to Him, this sovereign Lord,
We bring our hearts and minds and wills
That they, like him, may find new life
Amid those stark Judean hills.

And quickened, serve the one who came
To liberate and not condemn:
The Lord of *FAITH* and *HOPE* and *LOVE*
Whose star still shines on Bethlehem.

"The Good Old Days"

IN almost any culture you will find nostalgia for "the good old days." Time dims recollections of the way things really were. The fact is that every era has both its joys and sorrows, its triumphs and tragedies.

The time of Jesus, however, was an especially trying era. Rome dominated the known world, including the small province of Judah. In spite of this, the Jewish people managed to keep their own history alive. King Herod, who was faithful to Rome, carried out huge construction projects, imposed heavy taxes, and left the nation impoverished.

Many hymns of the Christian church tend to romanticize the birth of Jesus.

"O Little Town of Bethlehem" and "Silent Night" are so peaceful and serene. But the realities were much more harsh and unforgiving. Illness was common and life expectancy did not exceed the early forties. So Jesus was not a "young man" when he was crucified.

Peace, it seems, is not a given in any culture at any time. If there is peace, it must be within us, not necessarily around us.

SOME SECOND THOUGHTS

A day of peace? It used to be.
At least it always seemed that way.
Somehow the world seemed not so near,
So loud, so rude, and unrestrained.
The symbols of the season hailed
A simpler, gentler kind of day.
An air of quiet goodness reigned,
And innocence was not disdained.

Or was it really quite that way
In nobler times -- at Bethlehem, say?
Surely the world was loud and rude
Around the inn that Christmas morn.
No traveler in the throng gave heed
To where a pregnant girl might stay,
And bloody Herod waited word
On where his rival king was born.

The only peace the world knew then;
The only kind that it knows now,
Resides within some faithful heart:
A Simeon here, an Anna there.
So give us hearts like theirs, O Lord,
And guide our lives until, somehow,
The love of him who is our Peace
Is known to all men everywhere.

GRACE AND GRATITUDE

AUTHOR Anne Lamott has suggested there are really only two prayers, "Help me, help me, help me," and "Thank you, thank you, thank you."

An attitude of gratitude makes all the difference in the way we live our lives. Complaining works for a moment but doesn't sustain us in difficult times. G.K. Chesterton described gratitude as happiness doubled by wonder.

So it is that in 1621 the Plymouth colonists and the Wampanoag Indians shared a harvest feast and gave us Thanksgiving, the all-American holiday.

Isn't it curious, however, that Thanksgiving *precedes* Christmas, which is surely one of our major reasons for giving thanks.

A Season for Thanksgiving

How awesome is your universe,
O Lord, which has no end.
More awesome still your unexpected
Coming as a friend.

A friend whose birth and life and death
Have shown us that your care
Embraces every mother's child,
However unaware.

Your whole creation sings a hymn
Of unremitting praise,
Yet in your son alone we see
The purpose of our days.

So while we thank you for that orb
That lights the winter sky,
We thank you more for life in him,
A life that cannot die.

Because of him, the unseen order
Out of which we came
Now has a face, the face of love,
And dearer still, a name.

Because of him we also taste
The joy for which we yearn,
An earnest of that unseen world
To which we shall return.

And so we come at each year's end,
The transients of this earth,
To honor, praise, and thank you for
The world's Redeemer's birth.

THE MYSTERY IS – WHO WAS HE?

T HE central question of the Christian faith, a question theologians and lay persons have discussed and debated for two thousand years, is Jesus' question, "Who do you say that I am?"

The answer became more complicated after the Council of Nicaea in 325 C.E., the time, in the words of one book title, "When Jesus Became God."

Marcus Borg, in his book *Jesus A New Vision*, delineates and describes the various identities Jesus had in his own time. (1) Some saw him to be a *Sage*, a teacher of wisdom (he was called "Teacher" by his followers), who distinguished between the broad way of conventional wisdom and the narrow way of transformation.

(2) He was also seen as the *Founder of a Movement* to revitalize Judaism; his concern was the renewal of Israel.

(3) Further, as some of his disciples responded to his question, he was thought to be a *Prophet*, a forth-teller n the tradition of Amos, Hosea, Isaiah, Jeremiah, and others. Like the other prophets, he called on his people to *repent*, which meant to turn or return. Why? Because the Kingdom of God, the new order of God's sovereignty, was at hand.

Surely, Jesus was all of these things. The most important conclusion for each of us, however, is our own. How do *we* respond to his question?

The Question that Prompts the Quest

"Who do you say I am?" he cried.
The question never disappears,
Though countless answers have been tried
Across the past two thousand years.

"A wisdom teacher," some would hold,
And wisdom he possessed, for sure.
If not, would his stories still be told,
Or his timeless teachings still endure?

"A social prophet," others say.
A prophet? Yes, and clearly more.
Defender of the castaway,
Compassion's own ambassador.

"A gifted healer," others claim,
Whose mission was to make men whole:
To cure the deaf, the blind, the lame,
And gently mend the battered soul.

"A bold reformer," bent on turning
Israel, some say, to her call
To be God's lantern, brightly burning,
For the nations, great and small.

Surely the answers all are right,
These judgments reached by history,
And yet, somehow, they hide from sight
A deeper, greater mystery...

The mystery that a peasant Jew
Whose life -- and death -- disclose God's story,
Lives and reigns with the One who is true
As Prince of Peace and Lord of Glory.

THE SPIRIT -- A BIOGRAPHY

THE Spirit, a synonym for wind or breath (*ruach* in Hebrew, *pneuma* in Greek) has a Biblical history stretching from the act of creation in Genesis all the way through the Old and New Testaments alike.

Wisdom and discernment are gifts of the Spirit. Prophecy is a mark of the Spirit's presence. During Jesus' temptation and baptism, the Spirit descends to fit him for his unique vocation. At Pentecost, the Spirit empowers the community of faith.

The apostle Paul names the specific fruits of the Spirit, which he names as love, joy, peace, patience, kindness, goodness, faithfulness, gentleness, and self-control. And for the author of John, authentic Christians are those who have experienced a "second birth," the birth not just of the flesh but of the Spirit. While it would be foolhardy to describe any poem as a "biography" of the Spirit, this verse attempts to capture a few highlights of its history.

WHERE THE SPIRIT IS THERE IS FREEDOM

Creative Spirit, by whose hand all
things that are have come to be,
We bless you for your freedom,
ever fresh and ever new.
Like wind, or breath, you swept across
your whole creation, wild and free.
Like wind, or breath, our spirits groan
to find their home in you.

You called a people, small, unknown,
to be the heralds of your grace,
Freed them from their captors by
the power of your hand,
Swirled around their ragged band
across a trackless desert place,
Led them to a sanctuary in a promised land.

On lofty winds you lifted them through
all the trials of nationhood,
Whispered to them patiently in
times of peace and war,
Gently led them, freely fed them so
they lacked for nothing good,
Yet they spurned you, seeking other spirits to adore.

And so you sent your prophets, men
inspired by you to speak your word,
Messengers of mercy they imprisoned or ignored,
Leaving countless voices crying for
compassion yet unheard,
Leaving your own sheep without
a shepherd, or a Lord.

So, at last, you sent your son,
descending on him like a dove,
And resting there so fully that you
breathed his very breath.
You hoped we might discern, in him,
your steadfast, unremitting love,
That vibrant love that makes us
victors even over death.

Help us hear your call from bondage,
from our love affair with earth.
Cleanse our spirits so we're fit to live with you above.
Grant the glorious freedom which your
son described as "second birth."
Only with that freedom will our
hearts learn how to love.

Loneliness and God

S INCE we enter and leave the world alone, it is no surprise that loneliness is an inevitable part of the human condition, and perhaps the saddest part. Mother Teresa of Calcutta has said that "the most terrible poverty is loneliness, and the feeling of being unloved."

Most country singers would agree. There are hundreds of songs about loneliness, but country music is especially rife with heartache, disappointment, grief, and depression.

Who speaks to this condition? The psalmist looks to God for relief. Many psalms begin with a plea for help but most of them end on a note of praise.

"How long, O Lord? Will you forget me forever? How long will you hide your face from me? How long must I bear pain in my soul, and have sorrow in my heart?" Or "My life is spent with sorrow, and my years with sighing." But the same psalm ends with the words, "Be strong, and let your heart take courage, all who wait for the Lord."

WHO DRIES THE TEARS?

Who dries the tears
That come with days
Of loneliness and sorrow?

Who stills our fears
And lifts our gaze
To glimpse a new tomorrow?

Yahweh is His holy name,
The One who was, and is,
Now and evermore the same.
Both earth and heaven are His.

Who strums the wild
And mystic chord
That makes our heart a dancer?

An eager child,
With hope restored,
Who cannot help but answer?

Yahweh is this gracious Lord
Who names us as His own.
We know because we have his Word:
The Son who makes Him known!

TORN FROM THE HEADLINES

(OR TIMELY BOOKS)

Meet the God of History

If we say "Happy New Year" the first day of every January, what do we say when we come o a new century, or a new millennium? That was a question on many minds when we came to January 1, 2000. Some envisioned massive computer crashes. Some into the occult predicted this would be an "end-of-the-world" event. Most felt it was, at the least, a milestone in human history.

But few, we daresay, reflected on God's plans for the new millennium.

When the Middle East became agricultural four millennia ago, the gods of nature prevailed. But the Israelites were unique. They developed a faith in a God who was both concerned about and active in human affairs.

"I am the Lord your God," the prophets said, "who brought you out of Egypt, out of the house of bondage. Therefore you shall have no other gods before me."

A new understanding of the divine arose from this radical view of God as the Lord of history. Furthermore, this holy God demanded a holy people, a condition for which He would prepare them through the Holy Spirit.

Y2K

So here we are, the human race,
Our quest for joy awash in tears.
Six billion siblings called to face
The dawning of two thousand years.

What now, we ask you, sovereign Lord?
What trials or triumphs lie ahead?
Will new disclosures of your Word
Illuminate the paths we tread?

Good times abound for just a few
Now sated with the things they own.
But can it be while this is true
Your purpose will remain unknown?

New realms respond to our commands;
New disciplines we hold in sway.
With so much knowledge in our hands,
Has holy wisdom slipped away?

Like hapless sheep, we hunger for
The food your Spirit can impart.
From empty vessels do we pour
Unanswered questions from the heart.

So fill us now. Make straight the way
That speeds your kingdom from above.
Bring in the new millennial day
Of steadfast faith, and hope, and love.

SHOCK AND AWE

THE opening days of the Iraq war, given the intensive and unrelenting bombing of its capital, were described on television as "shock and awe."

That phrase was equally descriptive of the American public on hearing -- and seeing -- two hijacked commercial airliners fly into the two 110-story buildings of New York's World Trade Center the morning of September 11, 2001.

The aftermath of that terrorist attack was shocked disbelief at the first foreign incursion on American soil since Pearl Harbor. People needed to process the fact that we are as vulnerable as any other nation to the plots and plans of enemies across the seas. "Our lodgings had been rearranged," and, as a result, the following Christmas season was a time of grief not experienced before in our day. "Nine eleven" will be a watchword for our generation and perhaps for generations to come.

NINE ELEVEN (2001)

This was the year when grief moved in
And left our lodgings rearranged.
Nothing remained as it had been.
The furniture of our lives had changed.

No longer did we dare pretend
That hospitality could not fail,
That trust was mutual, friend to friend,
That human goodness would prevail.

The well from which we all must drink
Was poisoned, and the bitter taste
Clouded the streams of thoughts we think
And colored them with toxic waste.

Troubled and confused we turned
To other sources, deeper springs,
And in those soundings we discerned
More telling truths, more lasting things.

A loving God whom we believe
Will guide us home when we are lost,
A God who comforts those who grieve
And knows full well the dreadful cost.

A different future there will be
From all the times we've known so well.
This time, God with us, we will see
The meaning of Emmanuel.

WAR'S DECEPTION

FROM Augustine until now, there has been much speculation on the concept of the "just war," defined as one waged in a just cause, by a legitimate authority, with right intention, and as a last resort. For many, World Wars I and II were "just wars."

The problem is that such conditions are contexts whereas most wars are based on pretexts, Consider the "Gulf of Tonkin" incident leading to the Vietnam War or the "weapons of mass destruction" of the Iraq War.

Throughout history such pretexts have been useful because identifying a common enemy can produce social cohesion and because the myth of redemptive violence proves persuasive again and again. Indeed, for many who bond with their comrades, war is the "lyric moment of their lives."

The reality of war is different. Civil War general William Tecumseh Sherman had it right when he said "I am tired and sick of war. Its glory is all moonshine. It is only those who have neither fired a shot nor heard the shrieks and groans of the wounded who cry aloud for blood. War is hell!"

The verse *Alternatives* seeks to make the case for the futility of war.

ALTERNATIVES

War tells us it will make the world
a better place. It lies.
War multiplies and magnifies the enmities of men.
The evil war purports to do away with never dies.
It simply seeks a more expedient time to rage again.

We think that if we drive out evil,
goodness will increase.
But death cannot give birth to life.
This much, at least, we know.
The seeds of goodness must be
planted in the soil of peace,
Then cultivated, tended, and nurtured 'til they grow.

To choose the perilous path of war
should always give us pause.
No quest is less propitious than for war's unholy grail.
To think that we can deal with evil's
symptoms, not its cause
Is worse than futile and is destined finally to fail.

What war is really all about is garnering control,
The power to exercise our will so others will obey.
But only by example can we motivate the soul.
Apart from this, inspired by love,
there is no other way.

So in this season, in the face of war's unending lies,
We thank the One whose love for all His children does
not cease
For giving us a different kind of power to exercise,
The sovereign power of him who bears the title Prince
of Peace.

A Matter of Give, Not Take

I F our meaning lies in security, we will be on guard forever. The fact is there is no security in this life except the security we find in the Spirit.

That may be the reason we decide, when all else fails, to take a chance on love. Not the kind of love that clutches, or wavers, but the steadfast love of the One who will not let us go.

The Greek word for that kind of love was *agape*. And for this we need a model, an authentic human being such as the one who called himself the *Son of Man*.

Paul sought to define that love in his first letter to the church at Corinth.

"Love," he wrote, "is patient and kind; love is not jealous or boastful; it is not arrogant or rude. Love does not insist on its own way; it is not irritable or resentful; it does not rejoice at wrong but rejoices in the right. Love bears all things, believes all things, hopes all things, endures all things.".

This love, he says, never ends.

No Love Like This

He blazed a trail to go where we
had never gone before.
He led the way to love without
reserve, without return.
He knew how rarely we encounter
love without conditions,
And yet believed it possible for humankind to learn.

He based his word – and staked his
life – on one intrinsic truth
(Intrinsic but not commonplace,
as history has shown):
That those who give their lives away
will find their lives fulfilled,
While those who save their lives
will die unsatisfied, alone.

Convention teaches otherwise,
that *quid pro quo* is just.
No favor should be granted without benefit in kind.
That those who claim what's rightly
theirs will always win the game,
While those who don't collect their
due will wind up far behind.

But what a cold and calculating planet this would be
Without the kind of love that we
are called upon to give,
And what a calloused and conniving
culture we would see
Without some greater purpose than
ourselves for which to live.

Or we can follow him who loved
without equivocation,
Relying on the One he knew and
served and trusted then,
For if we fail to heed these "angels
of our better natures,"
Surely love like this shall never pass this way again.

WALKING THE TALK

"Not every one who says to me, 'Lord, Lord' shall enter the kingdom of heaven, but he who does the will of my Father who is in heaven." (Matthew 7:21)

Jesus may have been the first to distinguish so vividly between those who "talk the talk" and those who "walk the talk" i.e. those who actually do what they profess. In one sense, therefore, "truth" became not a word but an action.

California Episcopal bishop James Pike, in his book "Doing the Truth," summarized Christian ethics. But even the word "ethics," defined by Webster as "a discipline, system, or theory of moral values" can be misleading. For in the final analysis, a person's ethics are his or her behaviors. That, I believe, was Jesus' point. To state one's intentions to follow him is not enough. One must actually do so.

In our own day, many in the political arena, or more likely the politico-religious arena, claim to represent morality. We think that some "protest too much."

DOING THE TRUTH

"Moral values" seem to be the watchwords of the day,
And surely those who say they're
not important must be few.
But in the end it matters very little what we say.
What matters, and it matters
greatly, lies in what we do.

The prophet Micah said it well,
for those with ears to hear:
"What does the Lord require of those
whose feet this earth would trod
But to do justice, love kindness,
and with hearts sincere,
To walk gently, humbly, with a just and loving God.

How can we , then, pursue those wars
whose causes are not clear?
Or borrow sums of money we know we cannot pay,
To ease the burden on the few
who have no cause to fear,
And pass it on to generations on some future day?

How can we legislate the choices
women need to make,
Or foreclose the chance to cure insufferable disease?
Deny to some the health in which we all have a stake,
Or tell the children left behind there are no remedies?

If truth itself resides entirely in the things we do,
Our doing must reflect somehow
the things we're mindful of.
This match remains the measure
of an axiom that's true:
The only moral value of significance is love.

A Mixed Blessing

CHANGE isn't often welcome. It can be disruptive. It can also be a blessing. Blessing or curse, however, change is inevitable. This is not a static universe. And we are not static creatures.

It was said of Jesus, "He grew in wisdom and stature." At our best, we grow, as well. Certainly our understanding of faith does, as it did for the ancients. The theology of progressive revelation teaches that each new truth in the history of scripture supports, expands, and stands upon the former revelations of God's truth.

So if "the world is too much with us," remember that out of the exodus came Israel, out of the exile came the understanding that God had chosen Israel to be a light to the nations. Out of the crucifixion came the resurrection.

For all its pain, embrace change. The future will not be what it used to be!

THE GIFT OF CHANGE

The world is too much with us, Lord,
So many problems seem to press
Upon our ordered lives. A horde
Of changes brings us great distress.

Is there no drug to help redress
The fever of these times? No balm
To soothe the anguish, still the stress,
Restore the smooth and storm-free calm?

We seek your comfort, Lord, and yet
We're troubled, for we cannot see
How peace accords with Olivet
Or quiet calm with Calvary.

Or could it be that life is change,
That birth's travail brooks no delay?
That many things both new and strange
Are heralds of a nobler day?

Forgive us, Lord, for every prayer
That all the pangs of change may cease.
To make things new may be to share
Your burden, and to know your peace.

Security vs. Sanity

THERE was a time not long ago when nuclear war hung like Damocles' sword over our heads. There is less consciousness of that threat now. And yet the threat remains.

The U.S. has 10,000 nuclear weapons, Russia 16,000. Six other nations (Britain, China, France, India, Pakistan, and North Korea) acknowledge their nuclear capacity, one (Israel) does not, and Iran seeks to be a nuclear power. So the fear of a nuclear winter is still very real.

The policy of "MAD" (Mutual Assured Destruction) however, is nothing less than a death pact among the nations.

The day may come when nuclear proliferation ends and nuclear weapons are banished. In the meantime, what we have is hope, hope based not on human goodness but on the goodness of the Spirit to temper our decisions, lest we "become death, the destroyer of worlds."

THE LIGHT STILL SHINES

(IN A NUCLEAR AGE)

Can hope survive
The ghastly, godless games of death
That nations play?
We cannot say.
But blades that flourish in the Spring
Survive, somehow, the Winter's chill.
So if the winds of death are strong,
Hope's promise may be stronger still.

Can faith withstand
The terror-cloud that conjures demons
Up from hell?
We cannot tell.
But those whose faith is rooted
In the living God have come to know
That He is in the world, in power,
And that He will not let us go.

Can love endure
The threat of desolation that
Discredits care
And feeds despair?
Or can that love which conquered death,
New-rising from some empty tomb,
Dispel the paralyzing fear
And drive away the circling gloom?

The light still shines.
Make no mistake. Despite the darkness
Of these days
Its beacons blaze
In countless hearts and minds and hands

Whose love and labors will not cease
Until God's new creation comes,
And all his children live in peace.

ACTS OF GOD -- OR MAN?

"NATURAL disasters" are not entirely natural when human beings contribute so richly to their cause. Building cities below the level of the sea, despoiling the wetlands that protect those cities, and then building faulty levees, cannot be called ecologically responsible.

In times of such disasters, however, we would do well to remember that the English translation of the Greek word, "apocalypse," is "revelation," i.e. God's making himself known. And revelation cannot be rationalized or demonstrated, only received.

At the end of Jesus' "sermon on the mount," i.e. the collection of his sayings, he reminds listeners that following his words is being like the wise man who builds his house on the rock rather than on the sand, so it can withstand the rain and the floods when they come. That seems to be as true of cities as it is of individuals.

KATRINA

We greet each day that we survive
With gratitude to be alive.
The sun still rises every day.
The moon still holds its nightly sway.

But into quiet dreams there creep
Distressing thoughts that steal our sleep.
Our hearts have known for far too long
The temper of our times is wrong.

No levee holds the pain at hand
That floods across this troubled land.
Our whole world seems awash in tears,
And we are prisoners of our fears.

And so we ask, when visions die,
When truth is lost and leaders lie,
Is there no balm in Gilead?
No healing word to make us glad?

There is and if, in times of fear,
When heaven's voice is far from clear,
We listen, we will hear once more
Good news we have not heard before.

That he whom God alone could give
Has promised hope to all who live
That pain and death, for all their power,
Will not command that final hour.

So in this season let us pause
To contemplate the nobler cause,
The cause of serving with the son
Until God's will and work are done.

SIGNS OF THE TIMES

A<small>N</small> accurate reading of the signs of the time suggests that the world is now at a turning or tipping point. We are leaving the luxury of an age of domination and exploitation in which an economy of extraction and depletion has overwhelmed the environment in which we live and of which we are a part.

A consciousness is growing -- all too slowly -- that human beings are accountable not only for their own futures but also for the future of the planet. The urgency of an economy focusing on *sustainability* has begun to be taken seriously. But resistance to change is still rampant among those who profit from the status quo.

The dominant environmental fact today is that of climate change. Fossil fuel and agriculture have drastically increased the greenhouse gasses of carbon dioxide, methane, and nitrous oxide, and the radiant forces of these gasses are warming the planet.

The question is whether we are willing to take the steps to change our habits and lifestyles to meet the environmental challenge of our times.

TURNING POINT

The earth cries out for mercy,
Though its voice is hardly heard
In the pulse of poisoned river
Or the song of silent bird.

Diversity diminishes
Before our very eyes,
And yet we scarcely notice
When another species dies.

From the depths of ailing oceans
To the crest of mountain pine
The systems that sustain us
Are in radical decline.

The polar caps are melting
In an eerie global Spring,
While we purchase cars by tonnage
In a final fossil fling.

How lethal are the footprints
That we leave on paths we trod,
Oblivious to Nature,
And blind to Nature's God.

Are we not stewards of this place,
This earthly home we're given,
The one and only home we'll ever
Know this side of heaven.

Then let us choose to share the blessing
Rather than the blame;
Disdaining death, embracing life,
So earth can do the same.

HAIL THE ECCENTRIC

James Hillman in his seminal book, *The Force of Character*, takes issue with the fact that biology is destiny. Our destiny instead is to leave, as a lasting legacy, our character. He praises the value of our differences, even our eccentricities. And he notes that "Discovery and promise do not belong solely to youth; age is not excluded from revelation."

Taking to heart Hillman's comment that "one of the poet"s tasks is to bring a community to its senses," we have attempted to distill in these six brief stanzas the essence of his 220-page volume, which we commend to your reading.

In the 1946 Frank Capra film, "It's a Wonderful Life," George Bailey (James Stewart), on the verge of suicide, is shown what a difference his life has made in the lives of others and of the community. His was a legacy of which he was not even aware. The story of George Bailey is, of course, that of every man -- and woman. We do not know the impact -- positive or negative -- that our decisions and actions have made on those around us.

One thing is certain -- that he who never dares is unlikely to make a difference. Eccentricity may not be an immediately lovable character trait but it may also be the key to a truly lasting legacy.

Character

(Suggested by James Hillman's *The Force of Character*)

There's greater purpose in growing old
Than living long (a vacuous goal).
These vintage years were meant to hold
A work more worthy of the soul.

The work that still remains at hand
Is naming our peculiar star.
Reviewing life to understand
The character we truly are.

As youth *unfolds*, exploring ways
To help unveil its destiny,
So age *infolds* in Autumn days
To unveil eccentricity.

We would be different, if you please,
And lo, this difference adumbrates
Our nature, in a congeries
Of habits, attitudes, and traits.

With insight we may grasp, by grace,
This guiding force which wounds or heals:
The hidden form behind the face
Which time and time alone reveals.

Would we leave a lasting legacy?
To this then we cannot be blind:
Our real inheritance may be
The character we've left behind.

VIOLENCE REVEALED

RENE Girard in *The Scapegoat* and Gil Bailie in *Violence Unveiled* trace the history of violence back to the creation of human culture. Their conclusion is that every culture originates in an act of violence against a common enemy or scapegoat, which myth makes sacred. So they say every culture is the product of "unanimity minus one." And since history is written by the victimizers, not the victims, Howard Nemerov suggests that "the murders become the memories, and the memories become the beautiful obligations."

The Hebrew prophets, however, awakened empathy for the victims -- the widow, the orphan, the disposessed. They saw that their God identified with the victim. And this unveiling (or *apocalypse)* of violence meant that violence no longer produced order and unity, as it had, but rather additional violence. So the myth of sacred violence lost much of its power to unify.

The ultimate victim, of course, was Jesus of Nazareth, the perfectly innocent one whose death on the cross made the myth of sacred violence invalid. The result is that it's difficult these days to scapegoat anyone who is not a victimizer. *Time* magazine, in fact, has called our current age "the age of the culprit as victim."

As John the Baptist said of Jesus, "Behold the Lamb of God, who takes away the sin of the world."

The Scapegoat and the Lamb

(Suggested by Rene Girard's *The Scapegoat*)

No longer can the scapegoat be
The well from which our one-ness flows,
The storehouse of our harmony,
The ground from which our kinship grows.

No longer can the common foe
Sustain our sense of unity,
Rekindle order, or bestow
The blessing of community.

The myth by which we justified
The violence that made us one
Has quietly but surely died,
Its long and bloody course has run.

The leaven of the living Lord
Has risen, and will not allow
The mindless harvest of the sword.
The victim is the victor now!

The one we labeled enemy,
The target of our fratricide,
Now has a face, in which we see
The visage of the crucified.

The scapegoat has become the lamb
Whose death redeems us from the fall,
The faithful heir of Abraham
Whose sacrifice was once for all.

Abused for us, this blameless one
Has borne our victim needs away.
Praise be to him, God's favored son,
Whose birth we keep on Christmas day!

WHAT AM I TO DO?

DANISH philosopher Soren Kierkegaard, regarded as "the father of existentialism," wrote the following to his friend Peter Wilhelm Lund in 1835: *What I lack is to be clear in my mind what I am to do, not what I am to know. The thing is to understand myself, to see what God really wishes me to do: the thing is to find a truth which is true for me, to find the idea for which I can live and die.*

For Kierkegaard the central issue for the human being is the crisis of existence, which be wrote about in his *Concluding Unscientific Postscript*. His definition of faith is truth as subjectivity, i.e. truth as appropriation of commitment. It is not so much *what* is believed but rather *how* it is believed. Existence is realized when the individual chooses with a passionate inwardness. There is no objective or Socratic standard for this kind of choice.

Truth, in short, is paradoxical, concrete, and not universal.

This may be what Jesus meant when he said "Follow me," for "I am the way, the truth, and the life"

WHAT IS TRUTH?

(An Unscientific Postscript to S. Kierkegaard)

Objective facts like gravity
Can be observed or else inferred.
Such facts are plain for all to see.
Denying them would be absurd.

But facts and truth are not the same.
They come from very different spheres.
While facts are knowledge we can claim,
The truth informs our hopes and fears.

And truth we do not own at all.
That holy ground is God's alone.
If there's one ruling protocol,
It is through trust that truth is known.

That being so, we must conclude
That what is true for you, or me,
Will come from inward certitude.
The truth is subjectivity!

Yet unbelief remains uncouth,
And quits its quest unsatisfied.
It asks with Pilate, What is truth?"
Then promptly has it crucified.

So to the one who would be wise
To things above and things below,
We say, beyond all compromise,
We must believe before we know.

THIS IS OUR HOME

WE are not just our brother's keepers -- we are keepers of a place called home. This earth is the web of existence of which we're a part, on which we live, and on which all life depends.

Sadly it isn't news any more that every natural system in the world is in decline. And the lifestyle some of us have enjoyed for so long has been largely responsible for this decline.

Now a generation has arisen which is beginning to take seriously our God-given responsibility to be stewards of the "fish of the sea and the birds of the air and every living thing … of every plant yielding seed …of everything that has the breath of life."

If we have turned a garden into a rubbish heap, it is time once again to "let the earth be glad."

LET THE EARTH BE GLAD

Let the earth be glad for the work we do.
Let the earth be glad, and the people, too.
Let the gifts of water, soil, and air
Be those the whole wide world can share,
And let there be that equity
Which fosters peace and harmony.
We who are guardians, stewards all,
Of this green terrestrial ball
Are pledged to keep it (pledged and sworn)
For generations yet unborn.
So let us live in such a way
As to save tomorrow from today.
Let us bless this home we occupy
That what we treasure may not die.

Joy Comes in the Morning

Many psalms start with despair but few of them end there. Time and again they remind us that "Weeping may tarry for the night, but joy comes with the morning."

So it helps to remember in difficult times that "this, too, shall pass." Those who hope in God, we are told, will not be disappointed.

Maintaining that perspective is not a matter of will but of the spirit. Where the Holy Spirit meets our human spirits, there is always hope. And the two can meet only in prayer.

It is common knowledge that the holiday season for many people is a time of utter despair. Family and friends have moved on. There is nothing new to celebrate. But the cheer at this time of year comes not from our immediate circumstances but from the fact of Christmas itself, that God saw fit to come to humankind in the likeness of a child and that, thanks to his Spirit, we have not been left orphans.

A CHEERLESS FUTURE?

A cheerless future? Can it be
That all our dearest hopes are dead?
That progress and prosperity
Like early morning clouds have fled?

We mourn for broken homes and schools,
For leaders who are slow to lead,
For masters who misuse the rules
And traders mesmerized by greed.

Do all the footings we have laid
Lie shattered in disquietude?
Have all the fittings we have made
To bind the nation come unglued?

Or are these troubled times instead
The prologue to a greener day
When all have homes, and hope, and bread,
And strangers are not turned away?

Make no mistake. Our God is near.
His kingdom will not be denied.
His love will never yield to fear,
Nor will He take the skeptic's side.

So come in faith, be reconciled
To Him who is the Lord of all,
The one who met us as a child
At Christmas, in an oxen's stall.

Then shall his gracious name be praised
And we shall have from heaven above
The trust to take the trail he blazed,
The path of patient, trusting love.

Discovered in Contemplation

Feathers -- or Anchor?

THE author of the Letter to the Hebrews and Emily Dickinson agree on one point: that hope sustains the human soul. Dickinson put it this way:

"Hope is the thing with feathers --

That perches in the soul --

And sings the tune without the words --

And never stops at all."

In *Hebrews*, on the other hand, hope is described as the "sure and steadfast anchor of the soul."

While the Psalms are filled with hope for the individual , the Old Testament speaks of hope chiefly as Israel's hope in God.

Hope in the full Christian sense is encountered rarely in the Gospels but frequently in the Epistles. This makes sense since the Christian hope resides in the resurrection of Jesus Christ. Paul writes that "we groan inwardly as we await for adoption as sons, the redemption of our bodies. For in this hope, we were saved." He adds that "Hope that is seen is not hope. For who hopes for what he sees? But if we hope for what we do not see, we wait for it with patience."

What a contrast with our casual use of the word hope today. When we say "Hope for the best," do we mean anything more than "let's be optimistic?"

But such words can never replace the substance of our hope in God as we know him in the Christ.

HOPE

Hope is not like optimism --
blissful, warm, and bright.
It shuns the public square to sojourn
deep within the soul.
It drinks from springs of living
water hidden from our sight,
And gathers manna from a source
beyond the world's control.

The arms of hope reach out to
God, expecting to be fed,
Knowing that their expectation will not be in vain,
That those who seek the Spirit
by the Spirit will be led,
That those who ask in confidence
the Spirit will sustain.

We hope for things as yet unseen,
and not for things we see.
If perfect justice is our goal, we
know that we may fail.
But if we find the fortitude to labor faithfully,
We also know that in the end
God's justice will prevail.

Hope does not mean the end of pain.
In pain we come to know
The measure of the magnitude of obstacles we face.
Endurance is the only soil where character can grow,
And only through endurance do
we meet the gift of grace.

Our hope is not in anything that humankind can do.
If history is evidence, then history has shown

That what we know about ourselves
is true of others too,
Which means that we cannot rely
on humankind alone.

Our hope instead is in the One who
brings life out of death,
Whose gift of resurrection was
encountered with dismay,
The One in whom we live and move
and have our every breath,
Whose great surprise at Easter had
its birth on Christmas day.

A Deceitful Master

THE reason security is such a false god is because apart from the promises of the living God, there is no ultimate security in human life.

It takes time, however, for some of us to discover that. Our generative years are the time when we start to plan a secure, predictable life. We build families, careers, homes, and a status we hope will last us all of our days.

But one unforeseen glitch -- an illness, the death of someone dear, a great disappointment of some kind -- can make us stop and take stock of our goals. When that happens, we may start to trade the walls we are building for bridges -- bridges to others, to the world, and to our God who has waited patiently for his prodigal sons and daughters to come home.

The rabbi Jesus said it well: "Every one then who hears these words of mine and does them will be like a wise man who built his house upon the rock, and the rain fell, and the floods came, and the winds blew and beat upon that house, but it did not fall, because it had been founded on the rock."

WALLS AND BRIDGES

When we were young, we turned our minds
To building walls of many kinds,
Determined that those walls, one day,
Would be our tranquil hideaway

How hard we labored, and how long,
To make that refuge safe and strong.
We gathered stones from everywhere
And laid them up with loving care.

Until, at last, it stood complete,
Our secret, self-contained retreat,
Untroubled by the anguished cry
Of random strangers passing by.

But where no stranger's voice was heard
The air was still and no life stirred.
The peace we breathed with every breath
Was but the pallid peace of death.

And so we're learning, day by day,
To move those ponderous walls away,
To breach the gates of fear and doubt
And seek the unknown stranger out.

Where once we laid up walls alone
We now raise bridges, stone by stone,
And sometimes, on some awkward span,
We meet one like the Son of Man.

And find not just a footpath there
But something like a thoroughfare
Where those of high and low degree
May walk with equal sovereignty.

The bridges that we are build are frail.
The structures we conceive may fail.
But as we struggle, stone by stone,
We glimpse a plan beyond our own.

And thank the One who shows the way,
Who gave us all one Christmas day
His only Son that he might be
A Bridge for all humanity.

THE PATH TO MEANING

L IFE without purpose is empty. Every life needs a purpose to give it meaning. And meaning, in turn, depends upon one's commitments. It can be said, in fact, that the nature and quality of our commitments will determine the nature and quality of our lives.

For many, if not all, the ultimate commitment is self-giving love. Without love, in the words of the apostle Paul, we are "noisy gongs or clanging cymbals." Most of us know the Greeks had three words for love: *eros, philia,* and *agape.* It is neither erotic love nor brotherly love to which Paul refers, but the godly, self-giving love that has no conditions.

Another Paul, Paul Tillich, described faith as ultimate concern. "Man, like every living being, is concerned about many things, above all about those which condition his very existence. If a concern claims ultimacy it demands the total surrender of him who accepts this claim… it demands that all other concerns be sacrificed."

This is the premise of "Commitment."

COMMITMENT

What the heart needs most is one great love,
One passion, full and whole,
To quicken life, to stir the mind,
And galvanize the soul.

A love to which our scattered hopes --
Survivors of despair,
Can cling in yet unsounded depths
And find renewal there.

A love to which our lives are called
As to a holy grail,
A sure and steadfast love to take
The place of loves that fail.

And when we seek that love, we find
It's we who have been sought,
That what we strive so hard to buy
Has been more dearly bought.

So to this love we bring not just
Our frankincense and gold,
But all we have, without reserve
(What part would we withhold?)

By yielding all to this great love,
Our frantic search is stilled,
And in its firm and faithful grasp,
We find all things fulfilled.

WHAT HAPPENED TO THRIFT?

IF Benjamin Franklin was our patron saint of thrift, God is surely our model for extravagance. In God's economy, there is nothing wasteful about showering the world with blessings. On our part, such generosity should spur unending gratitude.

The fact is, however, that most of us seem to take most things for granted. Noting this, Meister Eckhart wrote: "If the only prayer you said in your whole life was, 'thank you,' that would suffice." G.K. Chesterton added that "gratitude is happiness doubled by wonder."

It was that kind of wonder to which Jesus pointed in his parables. "Consider the lilies of the field," he said. With such glory, he said, not even Solomon was arrayed. Or "consider the grass of the field, which today is alive and tomorrow is thrown into the oven…" His point was that if God is that generous and wasteful in nature, will he not provide his children with even more abundance?

Frugality has much support in the world. Profligacy, on the other hand, seems to be the *modus operandi* of God.

A WASTEFUL LORD

You know you're wasteful, don't you, Lord,
The way you lavish gifts on men,
As if life's cup were meant to drain
Just so it might be filled again.

If only we were more aware,
We might approve your spendthrift ways,
But how can we perceive, or care,
Who sleep through almost all our days.

We stumble through the world, not seeing
Half the wonders that we see.
We barely comprehend a leaf
And lo! We apprehend a tree.

From every race that lives on earth
You give us brothers to embrace,
And this before we've looked, in truth,
Into another human face.

And then, as if that weren't enough,
As if it all had not been done,
You let your love be crucified;
You give your own beloved son.

When love is spent so recklessly,
We know not how to count the cost.
We only know that all the love
We ever saved was really lost.

That's why we calculate no more.
To live must be to love like you.
So teach us, won't you, loving Lord,
Somehow, to be more wasteful, too.

Are You the One?

WHEN John the Baptist sent with a disciple from prison the question, "Are you he who is to come, or shall we look for another?" Jesus responded "Go and tell John what you hear and see: the blind receive their sight and the lame walk, lepers are cleansed and the deaf hear, and the dead are raised up, and the poor have good news preached to them. And blessed is he who takes no offense in me."

John had his own ideas as to how the Messiah should behave, probably with passionate judgment. Jesus' answer is that John will need to reach his own conclusion on the basis of the works that Jesus was doing, which were works not of judgment but of love.

As human beings, we are very much alone on this earth, caught between the twin mysteries of birth and death. But Henri Nouwen points out that we can convert our loneliness into solitude and that in such solitude we can encounter the living God, who knows and loves us better than we know and love ourselves.

No Longer Strangers

Once we were strangers, aliens all,
Unrecognized, unheard, unknown,
Between two mysteries held in thrall,
Summoned from birth to death, alone.

Then on the face of earth's long night,
Place of the silent and withdrawn,
A new and unambiguous light
Prefaced the swift approach of dawn.

And with that dawn, the dark dispelled,
The long expected day began.
And all who stirred from sleep beheld
The light which lightens every man.

The chilling night its course had run.
Its terror lay beyond recall;
For God had named one man His son
And, naming him, had named us all.

And by his power, death's prison clothes
Were stripped away and men walked free;
The crippled danced, and even those
Who had been blind from birth could see.

So let the new day's song begin,
And lift the one who still despairs.
We are no longer strangers in
The universe, but sons -- and heirs!

The Three Pillars

A SIGNIFICANT concept of our times is that of sustainability (from the Latin *sustinere* meaning to "hold up") The most widely quoted definition is that of the United Nations Brundtland Commission which defined sustainable development in 1987 as "development that meets the needs of the present without compromising the ability of future generations to meet their own needs."

Biological systems are sustainable in that they have the capacity to endure. They tend to remain diverse and productive over time, unless they are unnecessarily exploited. For human beings, sustainability is the potential for the long-term maintenance of well-being. This potential depends on three factors which interface with one another -- the social, the environmental, and the economic -- often called "the three pillars" of sustainability.

Given this interface, it is clear that humans as "co-creators" are co-responsible for healthy ecosystems and for social and economic practices which take these into account. The stewardship of resources -- human, natural, and financial -- will remain the key to a sustainable world.

ONE LORD, ONE EARTH

Creator Spirit, look with favor
On the world that you have made.
Pardon your rebellious children
For the reckless role we've played
As stewards of this wondrous place,
This great, green jewel aloft in space.

Teach us to become the kind
Of co-creators you would choose
To tend your fields and lakes and forests,
Mindful of the means we use
To feed and house ourselves, and share
The bounty of your loving care.

The earth is yours, no favored nation
Holds a special claim on you.
You love the Sahel desert child,
The mountain woman of Peru.
Touch our hearts that we may feel
The wounds that you would have us heal.

This season grant us grace at last
To learn to love this blessed sphere
The way he did who lived and died
And reigns to make this purpose clear:
Your work -- and ours -- will not be done
Until the whole wide world is one.

The Ultimate Paradox

The word *paradox* comes from the Greek *para*, meaning "beyond" and *doxa* meaning "belief." The challenge of a paradox is that it is beyond belief. It is not just a problem to be solved but a problem that challenges our assumptions and basic intuitions about the way the world works.

Jesus was a master of paradox, e.g. "He who finds his life will lose it, and he who loses his life for my sake will find it." His parables are laden with paradoxes. Cynthia Bourgeault, in fact, in her provocative book. *The Wisdom Jesus*, suggests that his parables are close to what in the Zen tradition are called *koans* -- "profound paradoxes (riddles, if you like) that are intended to turn the egoic mind upside down and push us into new ways of seeing." "This is a classic strategy," she notes, "of a master of wisdom."

The most stunning paradox, of course, is the humility of God. In Jesus, the apostle Paul writes, we find one who "though he was in the form of God, did not count equality with God a thing to be grasped, but emptied himself, taking the form of servant, being born in the likeness of men …" and humbling himself and becoming "obedient unto death, even death on a cross." This *kenosis* or self-emptying could hardly be more of a paradox for the sovereign of the universe!

PARADOXES

Can blest be broken, broken blest?
That thought dismays the human mind.
We only know that this is so:
The very life we lose, we find.

Can whole be shattered, shattered whole?
Such contradictions cannot stand.
Yet shattered men have walked again,
Restored, made whole by God's own hand.

Can strength be weakness, weakness strength?
A clear impossibility.
But lives reveal what words conceal:
God's grace attends humility.

Can suffering love be sovereign Lord,
A righteous king the son of man?
We do not see how this can be
But God, in Jesus, says it can.

THE GIFT OF FREEDOM

THE theme of freedom runs throughout both the Old and New Testaments.

It began with the release from bondage of the Hebrew people in Egypt some three thousand years ago. The Exodus experience not only freed the Hebrews from slavery but also established the covenant between God and the Hebrew people.

Freedom was reaffirmed by Jeremiah in the 6th century B.C.E., when he "proclaimed liberty" for any Hebrew still enslaved, demanding that Hebrews who had Hebrew slaves let them go.

Jesus, announcing his own mission at the synagogue in Nazareth, said that "The Spirit of the Lord is upon me … to proclaim release to the captives …to set at liberty those who are oppressed."

Later in his ministry, he announced that "If you are truly my disciples, you will know the truth, and the truth will make you free."

The apostle Paul continued this theme of freedom by stating that "For freedom Christ has sent us free," i.e. free from slavery to the Law itself, and so from sin and its wages death, which are closely bound up with the law.

Obligation has been replaced by gratitude; obedience to the law has been replaced by obedience to the Spirit, where freedom alone is to be found.

THE PROMISE

Lift up your heads. Be not dismayed,
My fellow-pilgrims, bent with care.
The world that pains us, chains us, drains us,
Cannot bind us to despair.

Awaken now and hear God's promise,
Made before the world began,
By Him who sees us, and who frees us
Through His son, the son of man.

Death no longer reigns supreme.
Its threats will prove of no avail..
The One who heeds us, feeds us, leads us,
Will not flee, nor will He fail.

Trust His word, the word made flesh
For all of us so we might see
That from death's prison he has risen
Once for all to set us free.

Christmas Break

We know -- or think we know -- what happened at Easter. But what happened at Christmas?

A child was born, for sure -- an infant boy. But how was this different from the birth of any other child?

Let the record show that God was at work in a different way with Jesus. His birth and life were distinctive from all the rest in history. Christmas was a turning point in the human race. A human being came into the world who grew up to reveal the nature and purpose of the living God first to his chosen people, Israel, and then through the work of the Spirit to a whole waiting world.

So at Christmas we come to the manger, to a cow's stall in Bethlehem, and there fall at our feet in worship to the one who saves us from every false idol we choose to honor in the world.

RESPITE

From the gods we manufacture,
From the empty praise of men,
From the myth of human progress,
Christmas saves us once again.

From reliance on our wisdom,
On our wealth and on our power,
Let us take an intermission
For this brief and shining hour.

In the manger, in a stable,
There was no great sight to see,
But the author of creation
Chose this lowly place to be.

Let us pause, therefore, in wonder,
At His simple mercy-seat,
And lay our worldly trophies
At the holy infant's feet.

And let us praise our Maker
For the one He sent to men,
By letting Christmas save us
From our idols once again.

The Way, the Truth, and the Life

I n the long history of humankind, no event has had the impact of the incarnation. The idea that a human being could ever reflect the wisdom and purpose of the holy God not only never occurred even to God's people, the Jews (who expected a Messiah who would restore the grandeur of Israel) but an idea that still confounds the limits of human reason.

Even more confounding is the notion of *kenosis* or self-emptying, i.e. that "Christ Jesus, who, though he was in the form of God, did not count equality with God a thing to be grasped, but emptied himself, taking the form of a servant … and became obedient unto death, even death on a cross." (Philippians 2:5-8)

The story has been told so often, and so well, that this retelling in a few odd verses cannot possibly do it justice. But it's told once again in the hope that it will further encourage our engaging in that same process of self-emptying which is both the aim and the result of "putting on the mind of Christ."

CALLING

Loving Father, Servant Son
What strange new work have you begun?
What destiny have you designed
For this your hapless humankind?

With what subversive kind of plan
Did you endow the Son of Man,
That he should walk this pride-filled earth
To give the humble second birth?

Shunning every self-conceit,
Drawing water, washing feet,
Risking scorn and ridicule,
He made life's lowliest tasks the rule.

Then, tasting every human loss,
He died, rejected, on the cross,
And showed the world to what degree
Your love will go to set us free.

Now, risen from a borrowed grave,
To reconcile, forgive, and save,
With caring arms that open wide,
He beckons sinners to his side.

But if we take the way he's shown,
And make this wondrous work our own,
One thing is clear: we need your power
To love with courage, hour by hour.

So guard us from the fear of shame
That we may glorify your name,
And give us eyes with which to see
Your own divine humility.

Then we shall live secure from stress,
And from the heart's forgetfulness.
Then we shall love and serve him well:
Our rock, our hope, Emmanuel!

THE HUNGER AND THIRST

"As a hart longs for flowing streams, so longs my soul for thee, O God. My soul thirsts for God, for the living God."

If this and other Psalms are indicative of the human condition, it may be true that we are *born* with a hunger and thirst for completion in God. And if that is so, why do we not spend our lives on our knees?

John Piper has written that "the weakness of our hunger for God is not that he is not savory but because we keep ourselves stuffed with other things."

But given the work of the Spirit, those "other things" never completely dampen the hunger we experience. As the apostle Paul writes, "When we cry 'Abba! Father! it is the Spirit himself bearing witness that we are children of God."

METAMORPHOSIS

Lord of life, we bless you for
The Word made flesh on Christmas day.
No gift was ever needed more
By children who have lost their way.

We bless you for the One who came
So every soul could know its worth,
And so your love would have a name
Above all other names on earth.

Your Word made flesh: what stunning grace!
No promise now is left unsealed.
At last, in this one human face,
Your power and purpose stand revealed.

And if in this one life we see
Your living word has come to dwell,
Then just as surely it must be
That flesh can put on Word as well.

That must explain this longing, Lord,
This hunger to be whole, and new;
To be transformed and, by your Word,
To have eternal life with you.

AGENCY AND COMMUNION

D AVID Bakan, in his seminal book on *The Duality of Human Existence*, posits that human beings have two basic drives, one for agency, the other for communion. As individuals we seek to have an impact on our particular world. At the same time, we seek to belong, to be with others.

In the realm of faith we are both agents and communicants. We are agents of a God who cares very much about each and every person on this earth. We are his muscle and sinew, his hands and his feet. To the degree we are faithful, we will be effective agents of God's concern and love.

If we are called to be agents, however, at the same time we are called to be in communion with others. At our best, in fact, our *agency* will serve the purpose of growing and nurturing *community*.

The world values power and we are taught from an early age to exercise our power. God values love and calls us from an early age to exercise love. In Jesus' example we find both -- a forceful, committed agent whose life and mission were focused on communion.

No Greater Gift

Work for peace but don't expect
The world to welcome what you're doing.
Look to God for hope to free you
From the shackles of despair.
Share the joy you find along
Whatever pathway you're pursuing.
Loaves and fishes, blest and broken
Multiply, the more you share.

Hold to faith. In all your trials,
As in your triumphs, persevere.
The fountainhead of faith is deep
And all who come may drink their fill.
Be strong and let your faith dispel
Those adversaries, doubt and fear.
The God of Abraham was faithful
Then, and He is faithful still.

Embody love. If any virtue
Crowns this fleeting life we live,
It is the steadfast love of God
At work, somehow, through one who cares.
There is no greater gift that God
Or any one of us can give.
The birth and death and life of him
Who came at Christmas so declares

Persistence Makes Perfect

WHILE the prophets spoke on a regular basis of God's impatience with his people, there is much to be said for God's patience with this world. No matter how long it takes, he seems determined for us finally to "get the message."

Jesus was asked "How often shall my brother sin against me, and I forgive him? As many as seven times?" Jesus answered, "I do not say to you seven times, but seventy times seven." In short, without limit!

If anyone needs God's patience, we do. And while the time to repent (i.e. to turn back to God) is always urgent, we can find hope in the fact that God still has hope in us.

HE COMES AGAIN

Out of a realm where love prevails
He comes, a king ordained to reign,
Into a world where justice fails
To make this world his own domain.

Not to the sound of trumpets blaring,
Not to the royal roll of drums,
But to a peasant-mother's caring,
Into an oxen's stall he comes.

He comes unbidden, unproclaimed,
Except by prophets long ignored,
To be a servant, unashamed,
And only then a servant Lord.

A Lord who comforts those who mourn,
Who sets the shackled prisoner free,
Whose spirit gives the spirit-born
A bold, divine audacity.

A Lord who takes on every ill
Of humankind, and every loss
And, bowing to his Father's will,
Accepts a cruel and shameful cross.

And though he comes and lives and dies
To bare the scale of human pride,
The One on whom his grace relies
Will not let death be satisfied.

And so until earth's final hour
He comes again and yet again,
Challenging terror, greed, and power
To captivate the hearts of men.

Challenging nations, great and small,
To forge a world where wars will cease,
Where men and women, servants all,
May build a realm of lasting peace.

THE INCREDIBILITY OF
THE INCARNATION

IT is not surprising the disciples were so surprised to encounter Jesus after his death on the cross. It is just as surprising for us to encounter him in our own time. Why and how should we be so convinced of his resurrection if it were not for the fact of the incarnation?

That possibility is anticipated in the Hebrew scriptures, especially the priestly literature, which emphasizes God's "tabernacling" with his people. And while the Old Testament may hint at its coming, the doctrine of the incarnation grew out of the early Christian community's experience of the presence of Jesus the Christ.

God was, indeed, "in Christ reconciling the world to himself." (2 Corinthians 5:19)

LET CHRISTMAS COME

Let Christmas come! How long it seems
Since last we heard the glad Amen.
Let trumpets sound the timeless themes
Of Advent's anthems once again.

Let Christmas come and let that morn
Illuminate the soul's long night.
Let hope be born as he was born
To flood the imprisoned heart with light.

We would not sentimentalize
The incarnation, nor deny
That in the manger, sinless, lies
The one whom men will crucify.

But in his life and death we see
A love which men cannot destroy,
And if we share his sorrow we
Will also share his perfect joy.

So let it come, that blessed day
When earth unites with heaven's throng
To praise him and prepare the way
For Easter's resurrection song!

THE MYTH OF REDEMPTIVE VIOLENCE

See any action motion-picture film these days and what you are likely to see is another stark example of *the myth of redemptive violence*.

Walter Wink in *The Powers That Be* writes at length about this belief, enshrined in history, that violence saves, i.e. that if we make war it will bring peace. He posits that this is the dominant religion in our society today, indeed the dominant religion of every domination system in history.

If our culture is awash in this myth, however, there is a counter-history of great force. It is called the Christian gospel. Jesus not only taught peace; he lived it, with incredible patience and persistence. "I have come to bring peace." "Go in peace." "Peace be with you." "Peace I leave with you." "As the Father has sent me, even so I send you…Receive the Holy Spirit."

This should have been the death sentence for redemptive violence. But the world has resisted the message and, in doing so, the Spirit. Only disciples of peace can change that, if we will, with the patience and persistence that come from the Spirit.

THE HOUSE OF PEACE

Is there peace at last? Can peace be won
With bomb and missile, sword and gun?
Or is peace a house we are builders of
With countless, nameless works of love,
Each plumbed with patience, set with care,
And buttressed all around with prayer?

If so, perhaps we must begin
To clear a place for peace within,
To strip away the fear and doubt
That shut the heart's compassion out
And tap the rock of faith renewed
In simple praise and gratitude.

Come, let us build, beginning now,
As God himself has shown us how.
At Christmas let us mark the birth
Of him who is our peace on earth
And look to him and him alone
To be our guide, and cornerstone.

OUR HELP IS IN THE SPIRIT

To confess in the Old Testament meant to acknowledge sin, either of the individual or of the community. Without such a confession, there could be no forgiveness by God.

The same is true to some degree in the New Testament, as in the people confessing their sins to John the Baptist, or as in the book of James who wrote "Confess your sins to one another ... that you may be healed."

More frequently, however, confession in the New Testament has to do with the confession, or profession, of faith. A typical example is found in Paul's letter to the Philippians, when he writes "that at the name of Jesus every knee should bow...and every tongue *confess* that Jesus Christ is Lord."

In the New Testament it's important to note, however, that it is only with the aid of the Holy Spirit that one can confess (or profess) that Jesus as Lord.

CONFESSION

We want to be seen as loving, Lord,
But the measure of love is care:
Care for the lonely, least, and lost,
The tested and the tempest-tossed,
And truth be told, we need to say
It's seldom that we love that way.

We want to be seen as faithful, Lord,
But the measure of faith is trust:
Trust in your goodness every hour,
Trust in your ever-present power,
But self-sufficient we would be,
And so we trust in small degree.

We want to be seen as hopeful, too,
But hope means being sure,
Sure as the rising of the sun
That your intention will be done.
Why is it, then, we turn from prayer
To doubt and to its kin, despair?

At love and faith and hope alike
We fail to make the grade,
Nor will we ever answer to
These higher calls without your aid.
We're wanting to be seen, it's true,
But not by others, just by you!

ONE WORLD IS COMING

"GOD so loved the world that he gave his only Son..." This well-known passage from the Gospel of John was not the first inclusive statement in the Bible. Eight centuries earlier, the prophet Amos said "Are you not like the Ethiopians to me, O people of Israel! says the Lord. Did I not bring up Israel from the land of Egypt, and the Philistines from Caphtor and the Syrians from Kir?"

Nationalism, the worship of one's own country, is like "Religionism," the worship of one's own religion Both impede love or concern for other *people*! Harvey Cox writes that there is not only more interfaith conversation today; there is also more conflict. "So we need to turn our attention to the religious dimension of political strife and the political dimension of religious strife."

A global civilization requires global dialogue. In the words of Hans Kung, "There will be no peace among the nations without peace among the religions." So we know where the conversation must begin.

Only when this is one world can that conversation end.

THE GREAT COMMUNITY

This warring world will yet be one!
No restive rulers can impede
The work the Spirit has begun
To unify this fractious breed.

From dark preserves of tribe and race,
From yawning rifts of pride and power,
The One who loves us, by His grace,
Has brought us to this hopeful hour.

And for the task that lies ahead
A people has been called, to birth
A less contentious time, to spread
Good will to all throughout the earth.

Good will that starts with dialogue,
And therefore cannot be confined
To church, or mosque, or synagogue,
Or single faith of any kind.

Good will that goes beyond the home
Of those we know who seek God's face,
To where the homeless nomads roam
Who make up half the human race.

Good will that, finally, is not bound
By party or by piety,
But reaches out, the world around,
To form the Great Community.

And some of us that call will find
(With power to help us on the way)
In one who loved all humankind:
The one who came on Christmas-day.

The Freedom to Choose

There's little question in the Biblical literature that human beings are given freedom of will, starting with the story of creation in Genesis, in which God tells Adam he can freely eat of every tree in the garden (except the tree of the knowledge of good and evil). And as Moses prepares the people to enter the promised land, he reminds them of their covenant with God and that they have a choice. "I have set before you today life and death, blessing and curse, therefore choose life, that both you and your descendants may live." It is also clear in Acts that human beings can "resist the Holy Spirit." (6:10, 7:51)

Freedom of will, however, is not freedom of the spirit. Jesus said to the Jews who believed in him, "If you continue in my word, you will know the truth, and the truth will make you free." They responded that they were already free. He said that everyone who commits sin is a slave of sin but that "if the Son makes you free, you will be free indeed." To be free, then, does not mean having the freedom of will to commit sin but rather to be free as a servant of God's grace and righteousness.

THE CHOICE

Humbly, simply, silently,
But surely, in that wondrous hour,
He came to grant God's amnesty
To those enslaved by greed and power.

Vested with his Father's grace,
He knew the cost of sin and pride,
Yet willingly he set his face
To suffer and be crucified.

But death cannot subdue the voice
Of him whose reign is from above.
To every age he gives the choice
Of tyrant-fear or servant-love.

And each of us must choose, my friend,
Between the plowshare and the sword --
To make of power life's final end,
Or walk beside a servant Lord.